Designing Effective Workshops & Teleclasses

7 PROVEN STEPS TO CREATING CLASSES STUDENTS WILL LOVE

KARYN GREENSTREET
SMALL BUSINESS COACH & SELF EMPLOYMENT EXPERT
WWW.PASSIONFORBUSINESS.COM

Designing Effective Workshops & Teleclasses:
7 Proven Steps To Creating Classes Students Will Love

For information, please contact:

Passion For Business Publications,
PO Box 331, Revere, PA 18953
(215) 485-0881
www.passionforbusiness.com

Although the author and publisher have made every effort to ensure the accuracy and completeness of the information contained in this book, we assume no responsibility for errors, inaccuracies, omissions, or any inconsistency herein. Any slights of people, places or organizations are unintentional.

First printing 2006

ISBN 0-9787010-0-3

Cover & Book Design by:

Jack Out of the Box Designs
www.jackoutofthebox.com

Words of Praise for "Designing Effective Workshops & Teleclasses"

"*Designing Effective Workshops and Teleclasses* helped me to take a closer look at all my programs. Karyn's practical, step-by-step system makes it easy to create successful programs, starting from scratch. If you have a great idea for a class but have felt stuck because you're unsure just how to put it together, then this is the perfect book for you."

— **Jim Donovan,**
author of *Handbook to a Happier Life*

"This book offers proven and instantly-applicable information, tips, and frameworks that are both cutting-edge and rooted in traditional research. It is a modern "how to" that is easily readable, yet packed with details that no workshop organizer can afford to be without."

— **Allison Nazarian, President, Get It In Writing, Inc.**

"I've always gotten great feedback from my students but after reading Karyn's book, I realize my classes could be far more effective following her suggested seven steps. If you're looking for a way to create effective and profitable training materials and programs, regardless of whether live, recorded, online or by phone, this book is the ultimate guide."

— **Bill Hibbler, owner, EcommerceConfidential.com**
and co-author of *Meet and Grow Rich*

WORDS OF PRAISE

"This book provides both novice and experienced instructional designers with practical techniques for workshop design and delivery. Karyn Greenstreet practices what she preaches by providing information that is clear, concise, specific, and interactive."

**— Barbara J. Lassoff, Senior Director,
Education Services/Quality Management**

"Karyn Greenstreet's positive attitude resonates throughout this book as it clearly presents the most essential points of workshop design. Even if you've never designed a workshop before, this book is presented in such a straightforward, motivating style that you're going to want to start giving your own classes right away."

**— John Marani, author, teacher,
and instructional designer**

"I've run workshops for over 25 years and found this book chock full of useful updates and ideas as well as proven common sense practices. If you're running a workshop and want to insure your success — don't miss it!"

— Nancy Baker, MCC, coach and mentor

Table of Contents

ACKNOWLEDGMENTS. 1
WELCOME 3
   Purpose 3
   Scope. 4
HOW ADULTS LEARN 5
   Andragogy, the Teaching of Adults 5
   The Three Stages of Learning 7
STEP 1 — CONDUCTING NEEDS ASSESSMENT 9
   Purpose of Needs Assessment. 9
   The Needs Assessment Process. 11
   Exercise — Needs Assessment. 15
   Analyzing Your Students. 16
   Exercise — Student Analysis. 19
STEP 2 — CREATING A WORKSHOP GOAL
         & LESSON OBJECTIVES 21
   The Workshop Goal 22
   Reasons for Lesson Objectives 22
   Crafting Your Lesson Objectives. 23
   Behavioral Objectives 24
   Examples of Behavioral Objectives. 27
   Exercise — Goal and Objectives. 28
STEP 3 — WRITING LESSON PLANS. 29
   The Importance of Written Lesson Plans. 29
   Components of a Lesson Plan 29
   Sequencing of Lessons 30
   Checklist for Lesson Planning 31
   Exercise — Workshop Outline 33

TABLE OF CONTENTS

STEP 4 — MAKING IT INTERACTIVE **35**
Creating the Introduction to the Workshop 35
A Note on Icebreakers. 36
Tips for Using Icebreakers Effectively. 36
Exercise — Designing Icebreakers. 38
Questioning: Your Most Mighty Tool. 39
Why Ask Questions?. 39
When to Question 39
How to Question. 40
Types of Questions 41
Sample Questions 42
Exercise — Create Questions 44

STEP 5 — DESIGNING EXERCISES **45**
Types of Exercises 46
Exercise — Create Your Own Exercises. 48

STEP 6 — ENDING YOUR WORKSHOP. **49**
Evaluating Your Workshop. 50
The Four Levels of Evaluation 51
Evaluation Methods 52
Sample Evaluation Form. 52
Reviewing Their Responses. 55
Exercise — Evaluating Your Workshop 57

STEP 7 — HANDLING WORKSHOP ADMINISTRATION . . **59**
Choosing a Venue. 59
Finding Space for a Live Workshop 60
How Long Should My Workshop Be? 61
Pricing Your Workshop. 64
How Much To Charge?. 64
When Offering a Free Workshop Works for You 65
Early Bird Discounts 66
20 Ways to Market Your Workshop 66
Handing Registrations 68
Payments by Credit Card 70
Sample Credit Card Approval Form 72
Payments by Check 73
Setting the Stage 73
Managing Your Student Communication 75
Preparing Yourself. 76

SUMMING IT ALL UP. **79**

ONLINE RESOURCES **81**

ABOUT KARYN GREENSTREET **83**

LESSON PLAN — BLANK FORM **85**

SAMPLE LESSON PLAN **86**

Acknowledgments

Many people through the years have helped me on my path to learning about exceptional instructional design and excellent teaching skills, more numerous than there is space here. To all my teachers, mentors, and training colleagues over the past 25 years, I send my thanks.

In addition, hundreds of thousands of students who have attended my classes, workshops, and teleclasses have assisted me in honing my skill. Particular thanks go to the students of my "Designing Effective Workshops and Teleclasses" course, who helped refine the contents of the class, and this book, over the years.

Special thanks go to my editor and proofreader, my mother and friend, Linda. Her insights and gentle corrections of this book have been invaluable. While we're on the subject of family, thanks also to my sister, Kathy, who always encouraged me to live to my fullest potential; my brother Lee and my father Roger, my steadfast supporters.

Finally, my profound love and deep appreciation goes to my husband, Alastair, who waited patiently for me while I wrote this book, encouraged me, brainstormed with me, and brought me endless cups of tea.

**"LEARNING IS NOT COMPULSORY
BUT NEITHER IS SURVIVAL."**

—W. Edwards Deming

Welcome

There are many reasons that students attend workshops, but the bottom line is the improvement or acquisition of new skills or knowledge, and how these relate to a better understanding of life and business.

By definition, the most fundamental judgment of the quality of any training program is the impact it has on the actual performance of students. If students cannot apply the information directly to their everyday lives, then what has really been accomplished with the workshop?

If done well, however, your workshops will sparkle and shine, and what your students learn will have a great impact on their lives and businesses.

Purpose

This book is intended to give you, the instructor, some useful "how-to" tips on designing and presenting effective training programs, as well as offering assistance with organizing, marketing, managing, and facilitating a workshop or teleclass.

You can use this information for live workshops as well as other types of training programs. We'll use the word "workshop" throughout this book to refer to workshops, seminars, teleclasses, audio programs, educational books and other self-paced learning programs, etc. (A teleclass is a workshop that is delivered over the phone, also known as a teleconference.)

In this book, an "instructor" is defined as an adult who teaches knowledge or skills to another adult. The "student" can be someone from across the street or across the globe. In order to avoid the awkwardness of using "him/her" in paragraphs, the terms "student," "she," or "he" are intended to be gender-neutral and encompass both males and females.

Scope

This guide is primarily intended as a practical manual for instructors. Therefore, the information on adult education theory will be brief. While there are many theories of instructional design, this book attempts to encompass many of them without rigidly adhering to only one viewpoint. The hands-on sections are expanded so that the instructor can learn new techniques for creating effective training programs. The marketing section is intended for those who market to their own in-house mailing lists, as well as the general public.

"LEARNING IS A TREASURE THAT WILL FOLLOW ITS OWNER EVERYWHERE."

— Chinese Proverb

How Adults Learn

Chemically, human brains learn the same way, and we all have preferred learning styles, whether we are children or adults. However, adults bring a special set of circumstances with them, which makes designing workshops for them a new experience for most instructors. You cannot rely on simply mimicking the lessons plans you experienced as a child; adults require more.

This section gives a brief summary of the current theories of Adult Education. It is meant only as an overview. For further study, you can do a search on "adult education," "instructional design," or "andragogy" on the Internet.

Andragogy, the Teaching of Adults

The term "andragogy" (a theory of adult education, from the Greek word meaning *adult leading*) was first adapted by Malcolm Knowles, a leader in the education field, in the early 1970s. The term contrasts with "pedagogy," or the teaching of children (*child leading*). Knowles set forth the following basic concepts:

- The adult student is largely self-directed and takes responsibility for his own learning as he takes responsibility for his own life.

- The adult brings his own life experiences to his educational endeavors and can be considered a resource in his own right.

- The adult needs to know why he is learning something.

- The adult learns best when he can apply the information immediately; he seldom learns simply for the sake of learning.

- The adult is motivated by his desire for greater self-esteem, self-growth, challenge, and recognition, as well as by a salary increase, a better family life, or to start or grow a business.

Adult learners also bring with them pre-determined beliefs and inhibitions about the learning experience and their own ability to learn, whereas children often have no pre-conceived opinions about learning. On the practical side, Knowles presents certain elemental conditions which are necessary to make the process of adult learning more "learner-focused":

- The climate for learning should be attuned to the psychological needs among students and instructors for mutual trust and respect, mutual support among peers, freedom of expression, and gratification from the learning experience.

- The learner should be involved in formulating his learning objectives and goals to fit in with those of the instructor. Participation in the planning of his own learning causes the learner to make a commitment to it.

• Finally, the active participation of the learner in the learning process and the use of his experience as a resource for learning are most important.

THE THREE STAGES OF LEARNING

While you can divide the stages of learning into many smaller facets, here are some basic stages that each learner goes through. Knowing this information helps you when designing your own lesson plans and exercises, so that you can take your students through these three stages when they are learning the material you are presenting to them.

1) **Readiness** — Get the students' attention and focus interest on the subject. Stimulate interaction with the material and topic as soon as possible and continue interaction throughout each lesson. Explain why the learning is important to the students. Let them know what to expect (agenda, objectives). Keep administrative details to a minimum (but make sure you cover the basic human needs: food, water, and bathroom locations).

2) **Presentation** — Keep good pacing of subject matter versus available time. Always plan for your timing ahead: allow enough time for each task without having to rush. Ask questions for feedback during the lesson. Use various methods and teaching aids. Use the students' experiences to make the learning relevant.

3) **Reinforcement** — When summarizing after the lesson, repeat key words and ideas. Use feedback questions, exercises, and homework (where appropriate), to increase retention.

**"WE LEARN GEOLOGY
THE MORNING AFTER THE EARTHQUAKE."**

—Ralph Waldo Emerson

Conducting Needs Assessment

Purpose of Needs Assessment

The very first thing to determine in your workshop planning is whether there is a need for your training among potential students.

You say, "What?? *Of course* they need it, and they want it!"

But how do you know that? Let's face it: why create a workshop if no one needs or wants to learn the skills or information you offer? What may have been a popular topic even five years ago may no longer be popular. (Never fear, many topics do seem to be perennial and will come back into vogue after a passage of time.)

Conducting a needs assessment helps you decide if what *you* want to teach is what *they* want to learn. Also, it helps you avoid presenting unnecessary training. If the topic has been wildly popular, there may have been many workshops already conducted. Is one more workshop really needed? Do you have new information about the topic? Is your audience new? Perhaps both?

This brings us to another very important reason for doing a needs assessment: to identify the target population. The target population is that particular group of people who would be most interested in what you have to offer them. Tailoring your workshop to that particular group brings you the most success.

Demographic trends can be discovered in a good needs assessment, as well. For example, the popularity of certain topics depends on the setting where the learning occurs — urban, suburban, or rural — and also in the country where prospective students live. Some topics may no longer be as attractive as they once were. A case in point is Native American Studies: once vastly popular in the United States, interest has now waned, while in Europe, it is increasing. However, business skills classes never go out of style, as does any kind of self-help or personal growth material. There is a perennial need for these topics across wide swaths of the population here and abroad.

Needs assessment also helps you to determine which sub-topics are of interest to your students. Asking a student to indicate whether she is interested in *"business skills"* may yield a "yes" answer, but when questioned more closely, you might find that what she really wanted was to learn about *marketing*, not *time management*. By doing a careful and precise needs assessment, you can determine exactly which topics the majority of students would like you to cover. This may lead you to create multiple workshops to organize these requests into logical groups.

Whether you call this a "needs assessment" or "market analysis," questioning your potential student base will tell you what they really want to learn and what they are willing to pay to learn. In the end, what matters most is what *students* want to learn, not what *you* want to teach them. Always remember to start where they are.

The Needs Assessment Process

There are several steps you must take to plan and conduct your needs assessment. By using this step-by-step approach, and reviewing the results, you can apply what you have learned from this process to your own workshop design.

Step 1. Appraise the situation. Consider carefully who your target audience is, where these people are located, and what factors are involved in contacting them to determine their needs. If they are geographically dispersed, you may need to use methods that allow you to communicate with them via email, online, or with paper assessments that can be mailed back to you. If they are in the same geographical area (for instance, if they are employees of the same company or members of the same association), you have the luxury of choosing other assessment methods such as personal observation and/or in-person interviews.

In addition to appraising your audience's geographical proximity to you and to each other, it is also important to get a sense of its potential size. Because it may be impossible to reach every individual person for your assessment, it would be more expedient to contact a smaller, representative number of people who reflect the larger audience. This smaller number is your "sample size." For instance, if you are creating a workshop for a 60-member organization, you could survey all 60 members. However, if your target audience is several thousand people, you will take a smaller sample of that audience for your needs assessment.

Finally, you need to determine how much time you have to conduct your needs assessment. Some methods yield faster results than others.

Step 2. Evaluate assessment methods in light of above appraisal. There are several assessment methods from which you can choose, and sometimes a combination of methods gives you the best results. Here is a quick overview of a few of the possible assessment methods available to you:

- **Questionnaires/Surveys.** You can produce either an online or paper questionnaire, asking your audience about their interest in the topic, and all the sub-topics you plan to cover. It is often helpful to ask them to rate their interest on a scale of one through five: one being "Least Interested" and five being "Most Interested." Make sure the larger numbers reflect the greater magnitude. You might word the questions something like this: *One a scale of 1 to 5, rate your interest in learning how to bake a cake at high altitudes.*

- **Interviews.** Like questionnaires and surveys, interviews provide a means for you to ask questions of your target audience in order to determine their needs and interests. Because interviews are verbal and can be conducted either in-person or over the telephone, you can also gather anecdotal information from the conversation that paper or online questionnaires seldom can gather. Typically interviews are conducted one-on-one. See "Focus Groups" for group interview options.

- **Observations.** If your target audience is geographically centralized, you can simply observe them as they go about their routine and make notes of where their skills and knowledge need to increase. It is important, however, to be as unobtrusive as possible to get a valid "take" on the situation.

- **Focus Groups.** Similar to observation and interviews, group discussions around a topic, guided by an experienced facilitator, can yield excellent brainstorming about what topics and sub-topics are of interest to the group. Keeping the group focused on the task at hand is necessary here as it is easy for a group to get off track during the discussion.

- **Media Review.** By searching through articles, books, studies, and reports, you can gain knowledge of the topics and trends that are of interest to the specific population that reads those documents. Included in a media review would be television shows, radio programs, and popular websites.

Step 3. Select the appropriate assessment method. Comparing the overall situation with the available assessment methods helps you to determine which method(s) are right for you.

Step 4. Design the tool. Once you choose the method (or multiple methods) you will use for your needs assessment, you must design a way to capture the information. For example, if you plan to use Focus Groups as your method, then you will design a series of questions to ask the group in order to get the information that you are seeking. Some methods require that you know, or learn, how to write good research questions, and there are many excellent books and classes on how to do this. After you design your tool, "pilot test" it on a small sample of people who are similar to your audience, to see how they interact with the tool. Notice if there is anywhere in the process that people get confused, often caused by language, wording, or misunderstanding what they are required to do. Make any necessary changes in your assessment tool after this step.

Step 5. Collect data. Next, use your data gathering tool on your entire target audience or a small sample of your entire target audience.

Step 6. Analyze data to determine trends. After all the data is gathered, it is time to sum it up. Look for commonalities in the answers that can give you insight into which topics students need and want to learn about. You may find that students have a wide range of topics they want to learn about, and this may encourage you to create more than one workshop around the topic.

Step 7. Develop a workshop lesson plan. After you analyze your data, begin to lay out your lesson plan outline, selecting your topics based on the results of your needs assessment and your own expertise about which topics need to be covered in this particular workshop.

Exercise — Needs Assessment

Selecting one of the given methods, create a needs assessment for your workshop. Determine how you will gather and analyze the data, and the timeframe for the assessment.

Analyzing Your Students

Once you have chosen the topics for your workshop through careful need assessment, it is helpful to learn a little more about your students. You may find that your needs assessment has answered some of these questions already, or that you still have a bit of detective work to do to uncover who your students really are.

There are three questions you need to ask yourself before you begin designing your workshop:

- What do my students *already* know? (Association)

- What do my students *want* to know? (Noise)

- What do my students *need* to know? (Objective)

Association is the "mental map" of relating new information with information your students already know. For example, if you want to teach your students about zebras, and they already know what a horse is, then you can associate zebra to horse. However, if they don't already know what a horse is, you have to take a step back and start with more basic information.

Imagine that you are teaching a cooking class on how to bake a cake. By knowing who your students are and what they already know, you can develop your lesson plan accordingly. If they have never set foot in a kitchen before, you'll begin with the basics. If they are experienced cooks, you will skip the basics and jump right into the intricacies of the specific recipes.

Noise is any internal or external distraction that keeps your students from absorbing new information. Imagine that you are beginning your workshop on a Monday morning. Students have just joined you after commuting to your workshop location. In their minds might be the following noise: Did I turn off the stove? Why did that guy cut me off in traffic? Will there be lunch served at this workshop? Where are the bathrooms? You can help alleviate this type of noise in your introduction, by giving them administrative details (food, bathrooms, and timing) and using a good icebreaker to bring their focus into the room and onto the topic.

When determining your workshop agenda you may find that students have a huge range of things they'd like to discuss. This can also be a distraction for the student, as they have questions about what topics *will* be covered compared to what *they would like* to have covered. Your needs assessment may have uncovered some of these possible topics. When designing your workshop lesson plan, you must compare what they *want* to know with what they *need* to know in order to cover the topic of the workshop. Here are a few things you can do to alleviate this noise:

- When designing your workshop, determine what they need to know (and the order they need to learn it) based on your expertise.

- Consider holding a different workshop on additional or advanced topics, so that your current workshop can be a streamlined and effective teaching environment.

- In your marketing materials for the workshop, make sure the workshop description clearly indicates what topics will be covered.

- When you get into the workshop itself, as part of your introduction and icebreaker, ask participants what they hope to get out of the workshop. When a participant mentions a topic that will not be covered, tell them so, which helps to manage their expectations.

Objective is your own evaluation of what they need to know. After all, you are the expert. You should have a sense of what skills and knowledge a student needs to master in order to completely cover the topic.

Other questions you can ask as part of your student analysis:

1) What is the size of the group?

2) If you're doing a workshop for employees of an organization, what level are the students in the organization?

3) How well do the students know one another?

4) How much time should I allot for the workshop (or for each lesson)?

5) Have I allocated enough time and space for their questions, and made it "safe" for them to ask?

Exercise — Student Analysis

1) Who are your students? Why are they coming to this workshop?

2) What are the key points/major topics your audience needs to hear? Are there logical groupings of topics? Do they cluster around a specific theme?

3) What do they want to know? Will you be covering these want-to-know topics in your workshop, or only the need-to-know topics?

4) What are the benefits (for this audience) of these key points/major topics?

5) What noise might they be bringing with them into the learning experience?

6) What is your plan for dealing with any noise that might distract the student from learning?

> "I HAVE COME TO BELIEVE THAT A GREAT TEACHER IS A GREAT ARTIST AND THAT THERE ARE AS FEW AS THERE ARE ANY OTHER GREAT ARTISTS. TEACHING MIGHT EVEN BE THE GREATEST OF THE ARTS SINCE THE MEDIUM IS THE HUMAN MIND AND SPIRIT."
>
> —John Steinbeck

STEP 2

Creating a Workshop Goal & Lesson Objectives

Once you have determined what topics are of interest to your target population, you need to develop the structure for your presentation. Whichever way you organize your ideas, you need a basic instructional tool: the lesson plan.

Every lesson plan begins with the development of a clear, overall workshop goal and specific individual lesson objectives. If you cannot communicate the goal and objectives of the workshop, you are not ready to teach. Workshop Goals define, in a general way, what students should know or be able to do by the end of the workshop. Lesson Objectives are much more specific statements of the outcome of each lesson.

The Workshop Goal

The workshop goal helps students to understand the purpose of the workshop. It is a high-level description of what will be covered in the workshop and what the student will know after completing the workshop. When writing your workshop goal keep in mind that the same text can be used in your marketing materials for your workshop.

Some sample Workshop Goals might be:

- This workshop is for new mothers to help them handle the myriad of chores and feelings that come in the first three months of motherhood.

- This workshop helps small business owners to write a comprehensive business plan and create a marketing strategy for the first 12 months of business.

- This workshop teaches students how to bake sugar cookies from scratch.

Reasons for Lesson Objectives

Lesson objectives create a framework for the design of your workshop. A good objective:

- Provides efficient communication

- Acts as a stimulus to thinking while writing a lesson plan

- Supplies a means to select appropriate workshop methods, workshop aids, and exercises

- Organizes the workshop

- Guides the lesson planning process, including topic selection, order, and teaching methods

- Tells the students what you can realistically provide for them and what they can expect to walk away with
- Acts as the instructor's accountability to the learners
- Enables effective evaluation

Crafting Your Lesson Objectives

It is important that lesson objectives focus on *what you expect the students to accomplish by participating.* Lesson objectives should describe clear outcomes for each topic, including any measurement of those outcomes. The objective must be in terms of what the student will know (content) and/or will be able to do (behavior) at the conclusion of the workshop, in demonstrable terms (called *behavioral objectives*). Write these objectives in a simple, concise format, using quantitative terms where appropriate.

You can choose to share these objectives with the students, or simply use them yourself to help in the lesson planning and evaluation process. With adult learners, it is often best to state up front what the objectives are. "At the end of this lesson, the student will be able to _____ ."

This gives them a framework — an outline, if you will — of what you intend to cover, and helps them prepare mentally for what lies ahead. They can also informally assess whether *you* met the objectives of the workshop by reviewing them afterwards. Did you teach what you promised you would?

Behavioral Objectives

Behavioral objectives explain what the student will be able to do (skills), or be able to explain (knowledge), when the workshop is completed.

Students should know the objectives in order to aid them in their attempts to acquire new learning or new insight. Knowing the objectives gives them clarity about what to expect in the workshop.

The following should be considered when writing objectives:

- What new skill, knowledge, or behavior is needed? (Separate *need to know* from *nice to know*.)

- What do the students already know about the subject?

- What will the student be expected to do with the new skill, knowledge, or behavior?

- Can it be applied immediately so that it won't be forgotten?

Objectives should always be:

- Measurable (able to be measured by your physical observation.).

- Clearly stated.

- Concise.

- Specific.

- Written with *action verbs* to eliminate broad interpretations.

The intent of your training should be communicated unmistakably to anyone who reads your objectives. This is called *objective measurability*. People should be able to measure, on the basis of your objectives alone, whether your student has absorbed the information you set out to convey.

Good objectives use specific performance terms, words which aren't open to interpretation. Writing objectives in this fashion is referred to as *behaviorally stated*. Here, for example, is an objective which could be interpreted in many ways:

"The student will know and appreciate duties required of him/her as they apply to the laser printer."

What is meant by "know?" By "appreciate?" Each person who reads the statement will have her own ideas about what the student will be learning. Other terms open to interpretation are:

- understand
- enjoy
- grasp the significance of
- have faith in
- believe
- appreciate

Active verbs are more specific words, open to fewer interpretations, such as:

add	describe	play
adjust	detect	perform
analyze	develop	recite
assemble	differentiate	remove
create	dismantle	repair
compare	draw	select
compute	explain	sequence
construct	itemize	sing
contrast	justify	solve
dance	list	state
define	make	write
demonstrate	measure	

Using words from the second list, we can make objectives more specific.

At the end of the lesson, each student will be able to:

WRONG: Know where the paper bin is located.

RIGHT: Identify the location of the printer's paper bin by pointing to it.

WRONG: Understand how to use active listening skills.

RIGHT: Demonstrate active listening skills by participating in a discussion with another student and accurately reporting back what you heard to your partner.

Examples of Behavioral Objectives

The following are more examples of precise, measurable (via your observation) lesson objectives.

Students will be able to:

- Present all the new income tax information to their staff and answer all questions concerning the new information.
- Meditate at least four times per week.
- Write at least one page in their personal journals after each session.
- Using the personal computer, the students will demonstrate how to code three website pages in one hour with no more than six coding errors.

Note: Always refer, again, to the objective after you've covered the material. This helps to reinforce the lesson and how it relates to the overall objectives of the workshop.

When you evaluate your own performance after the workshop is over (and you must do this), you may find that you did not have enough time to meet all the objectives you set out to accomplish prior to the lesson. If that is the case, you need to review the objectives and prioritize them. Perhaps you "bit off more than you could chew," and tried to cover too much in one workshop. Perhaps your students needed extra time with some of the exercises or discussions that you had not anticipated. You may need to divide your material into two or more workshops, or eliminate an objective that is not critical. As the instructor, your job is to streamline your presentation to make each lesson meaningful and useful to your students.

Exercise — Goal and Objectives

1) What is the overall goal, or purpose, of your workshop? Think about what kind of a workshop it is — informative: to share information, or instructional: to demonstrate or teach a skill? Or both?

2) What are the behavioral lesson objectives for your workshop? What do you want your students to be able to describe or do, at the end of the workshop? How will you test for this new knowledge or skill so that you can observe that the student has learned?

> **"LEARNING IS NOT ATTAINED BY CHANCE.
> IT MUST BE SOUGHT FOR WITH ARDOR AND
> ATTENDED TO WITH DILIGENCE."**
> —Abigail Adams

STEP 3

Writing Lesson Plans

The Importance of Written Lesson Plans

It has been said that if you don't know where you're going, you'll probably end up somewhere else. By writing out your lesson plan before you begin to teach, you are more likely to achieve your objectives. Finalized lesson plans allow you to concentrate on your *students* instead of concentrating on the material. The following will assist you in writing your lesson plan.

Components of a Lesson Plan

1) **A Title:** The title of the workshop and title for each lesson.

2) **Specific Workshop Goals:** The overarching purpose of your workshop.

3) **Subject Outline:** An arrangement of the content of your workshop into logical lessons. Includes major topics and sub-topics, in an abbreviated form.

4) **Specific Lesson Objectives:** Include at least one behavioral objective per lesson in your subject outline. Make them very specific. Have your lesson objectives prepared and in front of you while you write your lesson plan.

5) **Notes/Steps:** These are your "stage directions" — such things as the information you need to teach, questions you will ask, quizzes and exercises you will use, and time limits for all of these. Make sure you include a quick review at the end of each lesson before moving on to the next lesson.

6) **Materials and Aids:** Includes graphics, websites, student guides, reference manuals, and hand-outs you will be using. If they will be printed, make sure you know exactly how many of each you must have on hand for your class.

7) **Time Available:** Remember that the time available for teaching affects your objectives and, consequently, your lesson plan. Make sure you allow adequate time for each lecture, discussion, and exercise. If you're working within a fixed timeframe, you may have to shorten or delete some lessons in order to stay within the allotted time. However, if you are the one who decides how long the workshop will be, then you have more flexibility in the length of each lesson (and the overall workshop).

Sequencing of Lessons

The order in which you present new topics is important. Adult students learn best by stacking new information on top of previous knowledge ("association."). In addition, it is always important to do a quick review of existing knowledge before introducing new information.

When writing your lesson plan, look at each lesson topic and sub-topic. Are they in the right order? Is there a topic that *must* be taught first, before the others?

Checklist for Lesson Planning

Objectives

- Are your objectives stated in terms of what the students should learn by the end of each lesson?

- Are they stated in terms of what the students should do (an observable behavior) as evidence that they have learned?

Instruction

- Does your plan cover not only *what* you will teach, but *how,* and *in what order,* as well?

- Do you have an icebreaker? How will you get your students to start participating immediately? (We'll talk about icebreakers in more depth later in the book.)

- Has the workshop been sequenced so that "easier to learn" or "necessary before going on" material is given first?

- Are your questions prepared in advance? Are they mostly open-ended? (These types of questions draw out thoughtful answers from adult learners.)

- Do you have some examples that relate to everyday occurrences that the students are likely to have encountered? (Always be on the lookout for relevant news clippings or personal stories related to the workshops you teach.)

- How much time do you need to cover each major topic thoroughly?

Aids

- Will you use hand-outs, drawings, Power Point slide shows, stories, activities, and/or other aids to help get the point across? Have you practiced the activities ahead so that you are familiar with how they are done? (I suggest you use family or friends as stand-ins for practice when doing a new activity.)

- Do you have enough materials prepared to go around?

Exercise — Workshop Outline

Create an outline of all topics you plan to cover in your workshop. Make sure you sequence them in the proper order. Add timing to each part so you have thought through the time allotment. A hint: Don't rush your students through each section just so that you can keep to your schedule. Some parts of your lesson may take more time than you anticipated, but if your students are really engaged in a topic, you may want to allow extra time at certain points. Build in some elasticity.

Use the lesson plan form at the back of the book, or use the chart on the next page to jot down your lesson outline, objectives, and timing, and then transfer this information to the larger lesson plan later.

Lesson/Topic	Lesson Objective	Timing (including timing for exercises and discussions related to this lesson

> "I WAS BROUGHT UP TO BELIEVE THAT THE ONLY THING WORTH DOING WAS TO ADD TO THE SUM OF ACCURATE INFORMATION IN THE WORLD."
>
> —Margaret Mead

STEP 4

Making It Interactive

The mark of a great workshop is that it encourages student participation. Whether through an excellent opening to the workshop or asking questions throughout the workshop, interactivity helps build rapport between student and instructor, creating a vivid and powerful learning environment.

Creating the Introduction to the Workshop

- Is there an opening question or icebreaker activity?
- Does it capture interest and attention?
- Is it focused on the subject of the workshop?
- Is there a statement of purpose for the workshop?
- Is the workshop goal carefully stated?
- Is there planned interaction with the material?
- Is there an overview of what will be covered?
- Is there an integration of administrative details?

A Note on Icebreakers

As the name implies, an icebreaker is designed to start the process of warming up a group of people. Because an icebreaker usually initiates the official contact between the teacher and the students, it should be chosen carefully.

An icebreaker serves several important functions. It helps create a climate within which the group will work, and it also gives a teacher a feel for the group and vice versa.

Several cautions should be observed, however, in selecting and using an icebreaker:

- Don't get off topic. If the icebreaker doesn't relate to the workshop topic, don't use it.

- Don't use an icebreaker in which students could fail or be embarrassed.

- Don't use an icebreaker that will offend any person, even if that type of person is not present. Remember, the objective of an icebreaker is *to establish a climate of trust.*

- Don't let the icebreaker drag on. Once the point is made, move directly into the main part of the workshop.

Tips for Using Icebreakers Effectively

- Develop an environment conducive to group interaction by providing a common experience, or helping group members share their experiences.

- Never insist that students share personal information.

- If a student is taking too much time for a personal statement, intervene tactfully and put the group back on course.

- Determine the length of your opening activity by estimating the duration of the program. (A two-hour workshop would require only six or seven minutes for the icebreaker.)

- Consider your audience's expectations when determining the level of activity and involvement of your icebreaker.

- Select an activity that will appeal to specific kinds of audiences. For instance, one group of people might not be as receptive to an activity involving fantasies or imagination as would others. (This is where thorough student analysis is helpful.)

- Consider the background experience of your group and their cultural/gender differences when planning an icebreaker.

- Choose an opening activity that is appropriate for your particular students.

- Use an icebreaker as an opportunity for you to become acquainted with your group.

- Use the icebreaker to indicate what will be expected of the group and what the group can expect of the workshop.

- Use the icebreaker to show how *you* intend to participate in the program.

Exercise — Designing Icebreakers

1) Write an opening question or devise an icebreaker
   activity for your workshop in one or two of the
   following styles:

   Opening Question:

   Group Participation Exercise:

   Story or Anecdote:

2) Add these to your lesson plan

Questioning: Your Most Mighty Tool

Why Ask Questions?

- Questioning is the easiest way to get students involved.
- Questioning can help students understand, by making them think.
- Questioning gets students' interest and attention and can motivate them to learn.
- Questioning gives you feedback on whether or not students understand what you have presented.

When to Question

Ask a question at the beginning of your lesson to:

- motivate
- serve as an ice-breaker
- start a group discussion

Ask questions throughout your lesson to:

- draw on students' experiences or knowledge
- check for understanding
- keep interaction happening

Ask questions at the end of your lesson to:

- give you feedback on what learning has taken place
- reinforce the key points you wanted to make
- have the students summarize or conclude

Note: If a student asks you a question for which you do not know the answer, *always* find out the answer and give it to the student, even if you have to send it to them after the workshop is completed. Remember, your students trust you to know or find answers. There is nothing wrong with saying, "I don't know, but I'll find out and get back to you." Keep in mind, however, that with adult learners, someone else in the room may know the answer. Throw the question back to the group with a comment like, "That's a good question. Let's see if anyone else knows the answer."

How to Question

Write down your planned questions beforehand. Planned questions include icebreakers, discussion-starters, and feedback questions. Set them aside for awhile. After they've gotten "cold," reread them and ask yourself, "What misinterpretations of this question might someone have?" Then re-write to make sure the question brings the response you want. Plan back-up questions to bring out the main points or answers in case your first question doesn't work.

In a workshop, wait and let the answers come from the students. Don't panic if there is a long pause. Pauses don't always mean that students didn't understand the question. Pauses might mean that students are thinking it over, or are hesitant to take the floor. If you jump right in with a restatement of the question, or direct it to an individual, you condition the group not to respond to your questions.

The same holds true for questioning via an online message board. Ask the question and give students a chance to ponder the answer. Don't answer the question yourself.

Types of Questions

Open-Ended

Many different answers are possible. Open-ended questions call for opinion, views, feelings, or experience.

Example: What do you feel is a mother's most difficult task?

Open-ended questions are the most useful for motivating, drawing on experiences, and starting discussions.

Closed-Ended

There are only a limited number of correct responses. Closed-ended questions call for one-word or one-input answers.

Example: Do we offer a 6-month savings certificate?

Closed-ended questions are most useful for ending discussions and refocusing discussions. They may also be used for feedback. Closed-ended questions can be used at the beginning of a presentation, allowing the audience to begin to feel comfortable with their participation.

Group-Targeted

Asked of a group at large, for all to consider; anyone can answer. Also known as Discussion Questions.

Example: What are some cures for low morale?

Group-targeted questions are the most useful for motivating, drawing on experiences, starting discussions, and providing feedback.

Individual-Targeted

Directed at one person, preferably called by name before you ask the question.

Example: Barbara, what are some cures for low morale that you've used?

Individual-targeted questions are most useful for getting non-participants to contribute and to take the floor away from enthusiastic "over-participators."

Sample Questions

Questions that Motivate (Icebreakers)

What experiences have you had that demonstrate why it is important to learn about ____?

During the upcoming workshop, find the answers to these questions: ____

What questions would you like to have answered in the workshop?

Questions that Draw on Students' Experiences

What experiences have you had that illustrate the point we just covered?

Based on your experience, what is your opinion about ____ ?

Have any of you ever had the experience of ____? How did you feel? How did you handle it?

Questions that Start a Discussion

What points were made by this in-workshop exercise?

What are your views on ____?

What are the advantages of ____? The disadvantages?

Questions that Provide Feedback to You (to see if they understand what you have taught)

Can you summarize what we just discussed? What was the third step of the five steps we described?

Why was this important?

How would this apply to ____ or ____?

How would you solve this problem, using what we just covered?

STEP 4

Exercise — Create Questions

1) Write two sample questions for your workshop in each of the following styles:

Open-ended:

Closed-ended:

2) Add these questions to your lesson plan.

"TELL ME AND I FORGET. TEACH ME AND I REMEMBER. INVOLVE ME AND I LEARN."

—Benjamin Franklin

Designing Exercises

The purpose of exercises after each lesson is help the student cement in the learning by having an opportunity to practice and apply what they've learned so far. This helps to reinforce and test their progress with the lesson material so that you, as the teacher, can know if any lesson material needs to be reviewed before moving to the next lesson.

There are three criteria for selecting the right type of exercise: audience, objectives, and time available to conduct the exercise. This is where doing the student analysis, writing objectives, and writing out a lesson plan really pay off: helping you create the most effective exercises for your particular workshop.

There are so many different exercises to choose from. Of most importance, however, is that the exercise(s) you include must help you meet the objective of the lesson. Exercises must be relevant to the topic and useful to the student. In addition to determining the amount of time you need to conduct the exercise, also keep in mind that you must allow time for "processing" the exercise with group discussion and reflection after it is over. Don't rush this part — it is essential.

Types of Exercises

Below is a list of several possible types of exercises you can create, along with a brief description. Be creative and come up with your own exercises, perhaps combining two or more of the types below:

Storytelling/Story Writing — Ask the students to write a story, or tell a story, that reflects what they have just learned. The story can either be something they make up out of their own imagination, or a classic story, as long as they can make a correlation between the material they just learned and the storyline.

Brainstorming — Have the students work together in a group to solve a problem, weighing the pros and cons of each possible solution. The key to good brainstorming is not editing or criticizing people's ideas until all ideas are on the table.

Writing/Journaling — Ask the students to write their thoughts and feelings about what they just learned and how they will apply this new knowledge and insight to their life or work.

Drawing/Art Projects — Drawing and creating often brings out new ideas and new solutions that speaking and writing simply can't access. One possible idea is to have students draw sketches of their current situation, their future situation, or how they'd like things to work.

Questions & Answers — Create a series of questions that students must answer, either in writing or verbally. Ask students to share their answer with the entire class.

Partner/Group Discussion — Ask students to pair up, or form small groups, and then give them a discussion topic related to the material they just learned. Ask for one volunteer from each pair or group to share the results of the discussion with the entire class.

Worksheets — Give students fill-in-the-blank worksheets that they can use to walk through the material they just learned.

Role-playing — Ask students to take on roles based on the material they just learned, in order to practice a new skill. For instance, if they were learning about interviewing techniques, ask one person to be the interviewer and another to be the interviewee.

Puzzles and Games — Create or use a puzzle or game that allows students to interact with the new material. There are many off-the-shelf games, like Monopoly, that can reinforce specific skills.

Each One, Teach One — Ask students to form small groups, then give them a one- or two-page "lesson". One person from each group becomes the teacher, reads the lesson, and teaches the lesson to the rest of the students in the group.

Case Studies — Create stories or case studies for the students, where they have to apply what they have just learned to the hypothetical situation outlined in the case study.

Experiential Learning — Have the students physically do the steps to a project, to show that they can physically apply what they've learned. For instance, you can show them how to bake a cake, and then create an experiential exercise where they are asked to bake a cake themselves using the recipe provided while you observe them.

Exercise - Create Your Own Exercises

1) Indicate what type of exercise you will use for each lesson in your lesson plan. Write out each step of the exercise from beginning to end, and list any materials that you need to have handy to be used in the exercises.

2) On your lesson plan form, make notations about where you will insert each exercise, and the time each exercise will take, including any post-exercise processing or discussion time.

"IF YOU THINK IN TERMS OF A YEAR, PLANT A SEED; IF IN TERMS OF TEN YEARS, PLANT TREES; IF IN TERMS OF 100 YEARS, TEACH THE PEOPLE."

— Confucius

STEP 6

Ending Your Workshop

Planning for a smooth ending is just as important as planning for a good beginning. Your concluding remarks should reinforce the topics you have covered as well as direct the students' next course of action. This is a perfect time to allow for feedback from the group. What questions can you ask the students in order to review the main ideas of your workshop and gather from them how they will apply these ideas to their lives?

Be sure your closing remarks convey a sense of completion. Don't end a workshop abruptly just because you've run out of time or information. Students need to feel the workshop has come to a logical and emotional end. You may want to warn students that the conclusion is approaching when you begin to discuss your last topic. By saying, "We'll cover XYZ and then we'll be done," you let student know that you will be ending soon.

Evaluating Your Workshop

Evaluation is essential in order for you to improve your workshop and your presentation skills. If you are presenting a workshop in a physical location and intend to use a paper evaluation form, you may want your students to fill it out before they leave. Make sure you allow enough time for them to give thoughtful feedback. Consider whether you want to make the evaluation be anonymous, if you feel it will encourage their honest responses to your questions.

Your evaluation should contain questions only about things over which you have control. Asking them about the temperature of the room or the quality of the food yields you little information, as you probably already have an opinion about those things yourself since you were there, too. (However, if *you* arranged for a caterer, and the students were disappointed, you need to change caterers!) Instead ask them about what they learned, what was the best part of the workshop, how they felt about the interaction among the students, the pacing of the workshop, the "atmosphere" you created, what they'd like to see changed or added to the workshop, etc.

Design an evaluation form ahead by referring to your objectives at the beginning of the workshop and asking the students if they believe each objective has been met. (See sample evaluation form at the end of this chapter.) Also ask for feedback about the way you conducted the workshop, for example:

• Were they comfortable with the content material and how you presented it?

• What part of the workshop was the most useful?

- What part was least useful?
- What would they have changed about the workshop?
- Would they take a workshop again with you?
- What other topics would they like to cover in a future workshop?

There are several ways to deliver an evaluation form to your audience. You can distribute a paper form at a physical workshop, collect it right there or ask them to return it within a certain time frame. (Provide a stamped return envelope to encourage their participation.) You can also create an electronic evaluation form on a website, or send it to them via email. One great electronic survey tool is Survey Monkey (www.surveymonkey.com).

If you are offering any kind of "certificate," you can ensure 100% participation by asking them to complete the evaluation process *before* giving them their certificate.

The Four Levels of Evaluation

There are four different areas you can ask students to evaluate. Some are subjective (such as asking the students if they liked the workshop) while others are objective (did they learn what you intended to teach?). In essence, here are the four levels of evaluation you can use when creating the evaluation for your workshop:

Reaction: How well did the students like the workshop?

Learning: How much did the students learn in the workshop?

Behavior: Can and will students use their learning in real life?

Results: How does the training benefit the person?

Evaluation Methods

There are many ways to evaluate the effectiveness of a workshop. We are all familiar with the post-workshop questionnaire, but consider some of these other evaluation methods and choose one that works best for you and that gives you the evaluation information you need.

Questionnaires — used to get the reaction of the students to the material and instructor.

Feedback Questions — used during the training session to judge students' level of understanding, in a discussion format.

Quizzes — used during training to judge their level of understanding; this allows you to evaluate each student.

Projects — used either during or after training to judge transfer of new knowledge to new situations.

Demonstration of Skills — used either during or after training to judge ability to master a new skill.

Sample Evaluation Form

On the following pages is the workshop evaluation that I use when I teach the 4-week "Designing Effective Workshops and Teleclasses" course.

Class Evaluation -
Designing Effective Workshops and Teleclasses

Please rate your experience. Your feedback helps me to create the best learning experience possible for future students. Thank you!

1. Your Name (optional):

2. Can you describe the psychology of what adult students bring to the classroom?

    Yes   No   Somewhat

3. Can you formulate good lesson objectives?

    Yes   No   Somewhat

4. Can you use a lesson plan format to organize your workshop design?

    Yes   No   Somewhat

5. Can you create exercises for each lesson which help you to determine if the students learned the lesson objectives?

    Yes   No   Somewhat

6. Can you can accurately price your workshop?

    Yes   No   Somewhat

7. Can you effectively market your workshop?

    Yes   No   Somewhat

8. Which lessons did you find most helpful, and why?

9. Which lessons did you find least helpful, and why?

10. Did you participate in the full four weeks of tele-class sessions?

11. Were the lessons in the student material easy to read and understand?

    Yes   No   Somewhat

12. Were there any lessons that you would have liked to spend more time discussing in class?

13. What other topics would you have liked to explore in relation to designing workshops?

14. If you could participate again, what would you want me to do differently?

15. Do you have any other comments or questions?

Reviewing Their Responses

When reading evaluations, there is only one motto: "Leave your ego at the door. Open your Heart. Open your Mind." Most students are not trying to trash you as the teacher (although some *may* have an authority-figure problem), nor are they trying to trash your workshop. Their feedback is an important barometer that shows you where you might improve. Look for patterns to the responses and work first on the most consistent feedback that you get from the majority of students.

To keep this in perspective, here are some answers I got from a recent workshop evaluation:

Question: Was each lesson too short, too long, or "just right"?

Student 1: The lessons were a bit shorter than I expected, yet it was good material and the exercise portions helped to try to put the learning into practice.

Student 2: First one seemed too long.

Student 3: I am so busy right now in my business that all I could do was skim the material. I did find much of the material thought-provoking, and I was able to actually use a few of the techniques to check myself as I worked.

Student 4: For me they were just right. For anyone who wanted more, they could ask questions.

Student 5: I found it a bit overwhelming to have to do four or five or six lessons a week. I would vote for fewer, shorter.

As you can see, the answer was based on each person's perception, and there was no "right" answer. When I tallied up all student responses, 25 percent said "too long," 25 percent said "too short," and 50 percent said "just right," so I took that to mean two things:

1) Manage expectations better in the beginning of workshop. Let them know exactly how many weeks the workshop will be and give them an agenda of items in the beginning so they know how much material will be covered. It might have helped to tell them how long each lesson might take to read, or how long each homework assignment might take to complete.

2) You can't please everyone, but I had hit the average "just right" with a high enough percentage that I felt the material was the appropriate length.

Exercise — Evaluating Your Workshop

1) Determine how you will evaluate your workshop. Which evaluation techniques will you use?

2) Create a list of questions below that you would ask your students to determine the success of your workshop. Make sure your evaluation questions are based on the specific lesson objective(s) you designed at the beginning of the workshop. How will you be sure that all students succeeded in meeting the stated objectives?

3) Create an evaluation questionnaire to distribute to your students.

> "TEACHING SHOULD BE SUCH THAT
> WHAT IS OFFERED IS PERCEIVED AS A VALUABLE GIFT
> AND NOT AS A HARD DUTY."
> — Albert Einstein

STEP 7

Handling Workshop Administration

After you have completed the design of your workshop, it is now time to turn your attention to administrative matters. The first step is to decide where you will hold your workshop and how long the workshop will be. These two factors are important in the decision about what price to charge. Once you have these decisions made, it is time to market your workshop, accept registrations, and prepare yourself for the opening moments of your workshop.

Choosing a Venue

One of the first things you need to do is to choose the venue for your workshop. There are several different ways you can deliver your workshop:

Live workshop — delivering your workshop in person

Teleclass — delivering your workshop over a teleconference phone line

Email — delivering your workshop through written emails; this is typically text only

Website — delivering your workshop by posting the lessons on your website or message board; this can include text, graphics, audio, and video

Webinar — delivering your workshop live through a combination of telephone and web-accessed slide shows and graphics

Computer-based training (CBT) — delivering your workshop through pre-designed computer based text, graphics, animations, audio, and video

Audio CD — delivering your pre-recorded workshop on a CD

Written student guide — delivering your workshop through a book or manual

You can use any one of these venues, or combine them if it allows you to get the lesson across in a clear manner.

Finding Space for a Live Workshop

If your class will be delivered live, where will it be held?

While you can always rent hotel meeting room space, there are some other options to consider. For instance, Regus is a worldwide company that rents out meeting rooms and training room space for a fraction of the cost of renting the space from a hotel. You can find out more about them at www.regus.com. You might also check if there is space available at your local library, Chamber of

Commerce building, ambulance squad or fire hall building, community center, or church hall.

Finally, consider offering your workshop through your local high school or college adult education programs. They will provide you with the space and will market your workshop in return for a split of the profits. I have taught workshops through the adult education program at the local Community College. Twice a year, they send the entire adult education workshop catalog to every household in the county. That means that twice a year, my name is marketed to thousands of people, at no cost to me. Sure, I don't get to keep as much of the profit as I would if I did my own administration and marketing, but when you compare the costs, it is still less expensive to have your local adult education program do the marketing and administration work for you.

When doing a final selection of a location, ask yourself: Will the physical location where I am to teach this workshop have enough room and equipment, etc. or will I have to make adjustments ahead of time? Do I have a "backup" plan in case something goes wrong? Who will be on hand to make sure the place is set up properly and help me with any problems that arise?

How Long Should My Workshop Be?

This is a very big question, and there are several ways to look at it. Let's take each in turn:

- You can make your workshop *completely self-paced*, | allowing students to start and stop when they please. This is good if your workshop is strictly web-based text or in book format, with no live interaction with the instructor or other students. The downside of a completely self-paced workshop is that students often drop out mid-stream. It is also difficult to evaluate whether a student has achieved learning objectives, since interaction is minimal.

For this type of workshop, any number of lessons is adequate, as there is no time limit for students to learn the material. However, you may want to give them an estimate of what is involved in completing the workshop. Let your learning objectives help you to create an agenda that appropriately covers the material without giving the students "material overload." When students find the lessons too detailed, or with too much outside reference material, they tend to shut down and fail to finish the workshop. (This is true of all the types of workshops, not just "completely self-paced" ones.)

• You can make your workshop *self-paced within a structured agenda*, each week covering certain topics. Students receive and review a lesson each week (either in text, audio or video format), then participate in an online message board or group summary class or Teleclass call, where students can discuss what they've learned so far. In this way, students are compelled and encouraged to keep up with the material, and can participate as a group. This also allows for a certain amount of freedom, as they can review that week's lessons any time they want, as long as they complete them by the end of the week. You can see when someone isn't keeping up, and email or phone them privately to encourage them to continue.

For this type of workshop, anywhere from 4 to 12 weeks is appropriate. I have often found that students can not commit to more than a 4- or 6-week workshop, so consider dividing your workshop up into three parts: "introductory," "intermediate" and "advanced" workshops, if necessary.

For example, I have taught *The Artist's Way* in a live workshop format. For those of you who are not familiar with *The Artists Way*, it is a 12-week program. However, students almost always would begin to drop out around week 5. By week 7, I had to give them a "catch-up" week, as a break. It would have been better to divide the workshop into Weeks 1 through 4, 5 through 8, and 9 through 12, with a one-week break between each session to allow time for students to digest the material and refresh themselves before coming back for the next session. Built-in breaks can also help the instructor stay fresh.

- You can make your workshop *instructor-paced*, covering certain topics each week in a live workshop or teleclass. If the student does not attend the session, he/she misses out on the lesson and exercises. This type of structure offers more control and participation, but requires a higher level of commitment from the student.

For this type of workshop, a smaller number of weeks are appropriate. People are busy and have tight schedules. This type of workshop might be best done on a 1-session-per-week schedule.

Pricing Your Workshop

Setting a price for your workshop can be a daunting task. If you are doing the workshop inside an organizational setting, you may not be involved with setting the price at all. But if you are like most workshop instructors, you are selling your workshop to the public, and you must set a student fee for each attendee.

How Much To Charge?

Okay, so you don't want to starve to death to support your love of teaching. So what is a fair price to charge for your workshop?

Part of your pricing scheme has to do with how much student/teacher interaction your workshop includes. If you will give students personal attention, either in class or between class sessions, or if you'll spend time reviewing their homework assignments and providing feedback, they should pay more.

For an introductory-level workshop, a good starting place is $15 - $25 per hour, or $60 - $100 for a four-hour workshop. If the workshop skill level is "advanced," students should pay more. A professional-level workshop can range between $150 to $200, and more, for a 4-hour workshop, and I've seen 8-hour workshops as high as $450 for the day.

If you are a highly sought-after instructor, or have a high level of knowledge or skill in the workshop topic, you should charge more. If you underrate yourself and work "cheap," students will not take you seriously.

Check what other presenters in your area are charging for similar programs. Knowing the competition's price can help you determine what's appropriate and what students will pay. But there is one caveat: other people may have no idea how to price their workshops either, so do further research. Check your local Community College to see what they charge for their adult education classes. Contact professional organizations to which you belong to find out what the "going rate" is for training. There are many large training organizations that offer classes to the public and you can do more pricing research by looking through their course catalogs.

When determining your prices you must include your costs. If you are conducting a live workshop, your costs might include rental of the space, catering, handouts, and gasoline driving to and from the location. If you are conducting a teleclass, you may have to pay to rent a telephone bridge line and spend time editing recordings. If you use an assistant to help you with your work, part of the cost of your assistant should be allocated to the workshops you teach. If you accept credit cards, include the per-transaction costs in your workshop pricing.

When Offering a Free Workshop Works for You

Also consider charging nothing. Nothing??? Yes. If you want to do a pilot workshop where you will ask for in-depth feedback, consider charging nothing for the first one, and limit the class size to 10 or fewer students. It takes a lot of pressure off you to do it perfectly, and students love the opportunity to be involved with the birth of a new workshop. Also, if you are doing the workshop as a way to market your other services or products, a free workshop works wonders! The last time I did a free class entitled "Creating A Three-Page Business Plan," 207 people signed up … 207 *new* names to add to my mailing list, and 207 potential new clients.

Early Bird Discounts

Another great marketing tip: offer an "early bird discount" for people who sign up by a certain date. For instance, if your workshop begins on October 15, you can offer a discount of 10 percent to people who register before September 1.

Whatever discount rate you offer for the early bird discount, make sure it is enticing to people and that it won't break your budget. If you set the early bird registration fee too low, you could possibly lose money by not making enough profit compared to your costs.

20 Ways to Market Your Workshop

You have set your price, determined how long your workshop will be, and chosen a venue. Now you are ready to market your workshop. Remember your Workshop Objective that you wrote back in Step 2? You'll use that now to write some marketing text, describing your workshop topic and what students will walk away with. Once you've written this marketing text, you can choose from any of these marketing techniques to get the word out to potential students.

1) Send out an email to everyone on your mailing list.

2) Send out a snail-mail postcard, letter, or brochure to everyone on your mailing list who does not have an email address. Take this opportunity to ask them to email you with their current email address and update any other important personal information.

3) If you are part of an online mailing list discussion group or message board that allows commercial

announcements, announce your workshop there. These often limit such "promotional" announce ments to a certain day of the month, so plan in advance.

4) Check out the large websites in your topic area, and see if they have an events calendar.

5) Get your workshop listed on generic events calendar websites, like Seminar Finder (www.seminarfinder.com) and the Women's Calendar (www.womenscalendar.org).

6) Advertise in local newspapers, magazines, church and synagogue circulars, or other group newsletters.

7) Advertise in online classified ad services like Craig's List (www.craigslist.org). Craig's List is very popular (and free) and is organized by city, which allows you to target the area where your workshop will be held.

8) Prominently display the workshop information on your homepage and on other pages throughout your website.

9) If your workshop is being sponsored by an organization, ask them to post an announcement about your workshop on their website where potential students will see it.

10) Submit your website to all search engines.

11) Email websites that already link to your website and ask them to link to your workshop description page. You can find people who have linked to your website through Google, by typing in link: www.websitename.com (for instance, type in: link:www.passionforbusiness.com to find websites linked to the Passion For Business).

12) Put up notices in local food stores, health clubs, or retail shops.

13) Check out local events calendars in newspapers and submit your event to them.

14) If your area has a free events calendar magazine, submit your event to them.

15) Add to or prepare a separate Signature Line that goes out on all your emails.

16) Check out any local networking sessions, women's groups, professional organizations and Chambers of Commerce, etc.

17) See if your alumni association has an events calendar or mailing them send to past students of your college or University.

18) Don't forget your friends. Ask them to list your workshop on their websites, or to share your workshop information with their email mailing list. Have them send the email, not you.

19) Write articles for newspapers or magazines and include your class information in the "About The Author" box. Submit your articles to online article banks. Use your article in your own newsletter or ezine. (You can find a list of online article banks on my website here: www.passionforbusiness.com/a-lists.htm)

20) Form a strategic alliance with a colleague or company who works with the same target audience as you do. Ask them to promote your workshop to their audience.

Handing Registrations

Before offering your class to the public, you'll need to come up with a strategy for how you accept registrations. There are three things to consider:

Registration Process: decide whether students can register online, over the telephone, or via mail or email.

- If students are allowed to register online, you'll need to have a system in place to accept these registrations on your website, such as an online shopping cart system. Typically online registrations are completed with a credit card.

- If you allow students to register via email, it is wise that they do not email you their credit card information, as it is not safe to do so. Instead, offer them a safer way to give you credit card information, such as phoning it in, or faxing it to you.

- If you accept registrations by mail, you need to create a registration form that people can fill out and send along with their check.

Registration Form: determine what information you must collect on the registration form. Whether you accept registrations online, via mail, email, phone or fax, tell students what information you need them to give you. When your students register, make sure you capture the following information from them:

- Name

- Email Address and Postal Address

- Home or business telephone (in case email is not working)

- Cell phone, in case of emergencies

- Location (so you know what time zone they are in)

- How they heard about your workshop (to check the success of each of your marketing techniques)

Deadlines and Early Bird Specials: determine when the last date registrations will be accepted (or if you will accept "walk in" registrations on the day of a live event). Also determine if you will offer any discount given to people who register early. Indicate both of these deadlines on all marketing material so that people know what is expected of them.

Payments by Credit Card

If you are running a business, you may be already accepting credit cards. Credit cards are a great way for people to make payment for several reasons:

- People can take a class and pay for it in installments.

- People can sign up for a class immediately, when they first hear about it. Strike while the iron is hot!

- People from all over the world can enroll, because they will be charged in their local currency (it is deposited in your bank in US Dollars, or whatever your local currency is).

- People can enter their credit card information via a secure web page, which limits the number of phone or paper registrations you have to manually process.

- You know immediately if a credit card is rejected; with checks, there is a delay before you know if the check bounced, and *you* pay the bounced check fee.

- People can enroll right up to the first day of class, or if it is a live event, you can accept "walk-in" students.

Check with your bank about being allowed to accept credit cards, called a "merchant account." Or check out the many online merchant account processors that allow you to accept credit cards, often with lower fees than your bank charges. These merchant accounts allow you to accept credit cards online, by phone, or in person. Make sure your merchant account processor allows you to accept credit cards in all three of these ways, for maximum flexibility. For example, I use Practice Pay Solutions (www.practicepaysolutions.com). They often work with small businesses and offer both credit card merchant accounts and online shopping carts systems that you can connect to your website.

Online services such as PayPal (www.paypal.com) allow you to accept payments via credit card for a small processing fee. Because the student uses the PayPal website to process the transaction, you don't need to add a shopping cart to your website. However, this service may not be appropriate for you if you are accepting mail-in or walk-in registrations; check out PayPal's policies about how transactions must be entered and who is allowed to enter them into the PayPal system. Some people have reservations about using PayPal or giving their credit card information online, so consider having both online and mail-in registration available to students by using a merchant account to process your credit card transactions.

If you choose to accept credit cards for mail-in or phone-in registrations, it is always wise to ask students to fill out a credit card approval form so that you have their signature on file. These forms can be mailed or faxed to you, so include both your address and your fax number on the form. A sample form is on the following page.

Sample Credit Card Approval Form

I, _____ , hereby authorize Passion For Business, LLC to charge the following credit card account in the amount shown below for consulting services. This payment agreement will be in effect until services have been completed or are ended by request of the client either verbally or in writing.

Credit Card Information:

Card Type (circle one):

    Visa   MasterCard   American Express

Card Number: _____

Expiration Date: _____

Card Verification Number:* _____

Name on Card: _____

Billing Address (must match the address where the credit card statement is sent each month):

Street or P.O. Box: _____

City, State, Zip Code: _____

E-mail Address: _____

Cardholder's Signature: _____

Please complete this form and return to:

Passion For Business, LLC
PO Box 331
Revere, PA 18953
FAX: (480) 275-3321

* Your card verification number is your additional protection to ensure your credit card information is not being used fraudulently.

If you are using a Visa or MasterCard, please provide the 3-digit CVV (Customer Verification Value). This is the non-embossed number printed on the signature panel on the back of the card immediately following the Visa or MC card account number.

If your credit card is an American Express card please provide the 4-digit CID (Confidential Identifier Number). This is the 4 digit, non-embossed number printed above your account number on the face of your card.

Payments by Check

You can also accept checks, but the payment cycle is a little different. People will have to mail checks to you, and allowing time to clear means you have to set a deadline for enrollment. Check with your bank about fees for checks that bounce; with business accounts, usually the *business* is charged a fee if the student bounces a check (go figure!).

People sending payment from another country will have to send you a traveler's check in your local currency.

You may want to consider opening a local post office box for business and workshop registration purposes, rather than divulging your home address to strangers.

Setting the Stage

The first connection that you have with your students sets the stage for the rest of your class. Students are used to face-to-face classes, so participating in any other format, such as a teleclass, may take them outside their comfort zone. Giving them a feeling of safety and acceptance goes a long way toward their future participation and learning. To that end, here are some suggestions when starting a new workshop or teleclass:

- Send an email or letter to each student, welcoming them to the class, and encouraging their participation in lesson sessions (and the message board, if you have one). When emailing, make sure you put all email addresses in the Blind Carbon Copy (BCC) field so that no student receives all the other students' email addresses. It is considered a breach of online privacy to send an email to a large group of people by putting their address in the TO field instead of the BCC field.

- If your workshop is a live event, there is always the possibility that you will have to close the workshop in case of inclement weather. Give students instructions about who to call in case of inclement weather, to see if the workshop will be held or not.

- Ask each student to create a brief biography to share with the other students. Reiterate that no one is required to share personal information that they wish to remain private.

- If you are using an online message board, create a welcome message on the message board, and encourage all students to "sign in" for the class, introducing themselves, and listing what they hope to accomplish in class. Encourage students to ask questions. Reply to all welcome messages with a personal response.

- If appropriate, create an "agenda" page where students can see what topics will be covered in class. Also, list the objectives of the class so students know what they will be able to achieve by the end of the workshop.

- Create a short biography of yourself, including a picture. You may already have this on your website. If you have an assistant or coordinator, introduce him/her as well.

- Learn the students' names, and always call students by name.

- Message boards almost always encourage the learner to higher levels of thought because they have more time to think and write a response. Try to give well-thought out responses to their posts, when possible and appropriate. Encourage them when they have a good answer, and ask leading questions that help them think further when necessary.

Managing Your Student Communication

Once students have registered for your workshop, it is important to keep in touch with throughout the duration of the workshop. There are several psychological reasons for this:

- First, it makes the student feel as if you are paying individual attention to her, which encourages her to continue.

- Second, it offers the student an opportunity to communicate with you privately if there are problems or questions.

- Third, it encourages the student to participate, as it reminds her that others are participating as well.

The easiest way to keep in contact with students is via email. If your email program allows you, create a separate "address book" or "contact list" of just the students for that workshop, or put them in a "group" in your address book. This makes mass-emailing easier, and allows you to see your complete student list at a glance. You may want to print out this list and take it to your workshop, to be used for attendance records.

Preparing Yourself

Before you actually conduct your workshop, it is important that you prepare yourself. While good teaching and presentation skills are important, nothing goes farther than practicing your workshop, out loud, all the way through, over and over again. You may want to practice in front of a group of volunteers (and ask them for feedback), or simply rope family and friends into listening to portions of your workshop. This practicing will help you nail down timing of each lesson and exercise, and help you to formulate the words you will use in your lessons, and therefore be less nervous when delivering your workshop.

In addition to practicing your workshop, you might want to create a list of handouts and supplies you will need. This way, you won't forget anything during the final rushing hours before the first day of class. If it is a live presentation, make sure your list includes these items:

- Business cards
- Notepads, pens (for you and for your students)
- Flip chart markers and/or dry erase markers for whiteboards

- Laptop and Power Point slideshow, if you are using one
- Power strips and extension cords
- Handouts, workbooks, and other printed student materials
- Credit card processing forms, if you are accepting walk-in registrations
- Student list and all their phone numbers, in case of emergencies
- Contact and driving information for the venue
- Masking tape or duct tape (you'd be surprised what you can fix with a bit of tape)
- Tissues, breath mints, and other personal items
- Tape recorder or digital recorder, if you are going to record the audio from your workshop
- Name tags and markers (or print them in advance)

Summing It All Up

By now you should know the basics of designing a workshop, from icebreakers to evaluation. You've had some experience with how to price and market your workshop.

The only thing left now is to DO IT! Choose a topic that you are passionate about, and go out there and teach it to the entire world!

I wish you the greatest good luck and success with your teaching adventures.

With Warmest Regards,

Karyn

Karyn Greenstreet

Passion For Business LLC
"Empowering The Self Employed To Succeed"
www.PassionForBusiness.com

Online Resources

Resources in This Book — The Internet changes quickly, and some of the online resources I have mentioned in this book may no longer be available. For the most recent list of resources about instructional design and administering your workshop, visit our website: www.passionforbusiness.com/dewt-resources.htm

Take The Class! — I teach *Designing Effective Workshop* and Teleclasses every four months via teleclass format. This class helps you to apply everything you learn in this book to your own workshop design project, and finish your workshop lesson plan by the end of class. To learn more about this class and to register for the next one, visit our Calendar of Events: www.passionforbusiness.com/calendar.htm

Self Employed Success Ezine — I write a monthly email newsletter for self-employed small business owners, offering tips and techniques to grow their businesses. To subscribe, visit our website: www.passionforbusiness.com

About Karyn Greenstreet

Karyn Greenstreet is an internationally-known self-employment expert, speaker and author with 25 years of self-employment and instructional design experience. She has taught personal growth and business topics to over 250,000 people worldwide and is extraordinarily passionate about helping self-employed people to create the life and business they want. She is the President of Passion For Business LLC.

Karyn also owns The Success Alliance — a mastermind group for self-employed people, Taming The Technology Tiger — a website that helps self-employed people use technology to run their business, and Self Employed Woman — a community-based website for self-employed women, where they can ask for support, brainstorm, network, and share the ups and downs of self-employment.

Karyn has been on the teaching faculty of several schools, where she taught classes in starting and running small businesses. She has written over 50 student guides on many topics: personal growth, success and motivation, spirituality, business skills, and software education.

She is featured in the book, *Growing Your Business with Google for Dummies* by Brad Hill, in Entrepreneur Magazine in the article *"What's Love Got to Do With It?"* by Judith Potwora, and in American Express Ventures Magazine. Karyn is a contributing author to two books: *Streetwise Small Business Book of Lists* by Gene Marks, and Bill Hibbler and Joe Vitale's book on mastermind groups, *Meet and Grow Rich.*

Karyn holds a Bachelor of Science degree in Business Administration and Management, is certified in Adult Education Design and Implementation, and has done post-graduate work in Business Administration and Computer Systems. She is a graduate of the 125-hour CoachU coach training program.

Areas of Expertise:

- Starting and Managing a Small Business
- Creative Marketing and Branding
- Website Design and Usability
- Getting High Rankings on Search Engines
- Marketing on the Internet
- Using Technology to Increase Efficiency and Productivity
- Balancing Work and Personal Life
- Time Management
- Becoming More Organized and Productive
- Personal Success and Motivation

LESSON PLAN — BLANK FORM

Date Modified:
Workshop Goal:

Workshop Title:

Outline/Topic	Lesson Objective	Training Notes, Questions, Resources, Exercises	Timing

SAMPLE LESSON PLAN

Workshop Title: "How to Bake Grandma Snook's Sugar Cookies" Class

Date Modified: 12/25/01 — Page 1

Workshop Goal: Students will be able to read the recipe, gather and measure ingredients, combine ingredients, and properly bake the cookies.

Outline/Topic	Lesson Objective	Training Notes, Questions, Resources, Exercises	Timing
Introduction	Set the stage for the class; answer any administrative questions	• Introduce myself • Introduce the workshop agenda • Find out students' previous baking experience • Distribute recipe cards	5 minutes
Step 1 — Reading The Recipe	Students will be able to demonstrate that they can read the recipe by gathering the appropriate ingredients on their work tables. Explain the order in which recipes are written	• Review this particular recipe's order • Explain about pre-heating instructions • Explain the importance of gathering all ingredients before measuring and mixing • Exercise — ask students to read the recipe and gather the ingredients from the storage areas. • Exercise — ask students to pre-heat their ovens	15 minutes
Step 2 — Measuring the Ingredients	Students will be able to demonstrate how to measure each ingredient using the proper measuring device	• Explain the difference between liquid and solid measurements • Explain how to measure liquids using the appropriate measuring cup and measuring spoons • Explain how to measure solids using appropriate measuring cups, measuring spoons and weight scale • Exercise — ask students to measure out the ingredients using the appropriate measuring device	15 minutes